Our Mother of Sorrows

by Nina Clements

Crossroads Poetry Series
Three Fires Confederacy
Waawiiyaatanong ✛ Windsor, ON

First Edition. August 2020

Library and Archives Canada Cataloguing in Publication

Title: Our mother of sorrows / by Nina Clements.

Names: Clements, Nina, 1979- author.

Description: First edition. | Poems.

Identifiers: Canadiana 20200251589 | ISBN 9781988214405 (paperback)

Classification: LCC PS3603.L46 O97 2020 | DDC 811/.6—dc23

Book cover design: D.A. Lockhart
Cover Image: Stacy Russo
Book layout: D.A. Lockhart

Published in the United States of America and Canada by

 Urban Farmhouse Press
www.urbanfarmhousepress.ca

The Crossroads Poetry Series is a line of books that showcases established and emerging poetic voices from across North America. The books in this series represent what the editors at UFP believe to be some of the strongest voices in both American and Canadian poetics.

Printed in Chaparral Pro

Contents

For my sisters,
Annette and Lisa.

Three Sisters

It was her knees I loved,
cheek against the rough ridge.
I rubbed my face into them.
She sat there smoking, picking
her feet only sometimes. But I loved
the rough little hairs—the tiniest
spikes against my skin.
I wanted to break a wedge
of Parmesan against those knees.
I sat on the carpet and breathed in smoke.

There was always some man lying
on the television screen. I remembered
Oliver North, but I remembered his beautiful
secretary more. She could not recall anything.
The transcripts were always expletive deleted.
Mommy, what's an expletive? I understood
deleting—just another way to disappear.
Daddy became a liar, but he wasn't on TV.
It's been many years since I learned
how the expletives fled.
All those words like polished
glass, begging to be read.

We watched old movies.
Pollyanna. Mary Poppins.
Oh, the absent father.
Ours appeared each day at
4:00, home from the railroad,
in no mood for high-pitched
songs and chatter. He came
upon our picnic underneath
the table—rounds
of pepperoni atop Ritz crackers.
The chewy crunch of it, the salted
fat smeared on our lips. He did not
understand what had happened
to dinner. We did not understand
he had lost his job, that men had taken
money. All he wanted
was to sit at the dining room table
with his pork chop, thinking
of what to do. He wanted the quiet.
She could only provide the chaos.

She didn't beat us
with hangers. Her hands
were good enough,
but only when we
deserved it. And children
do deserve
so much. She clattered
the hangers, muttering as
she hung up clothes
in the room three of us
shared—a small
room in an even smaller house.
She clattered the hangers and
turned, then her hands
were on me. I had said something
ungrateful. I only remember
the sting.

Three little girls who lived,
each one quick after
the other. After the first
baby, who died.
And Dad had lost
his job, and Mommy
did not work, except
on Saturday nights,
for the JC Penney catalog.
So Dad took us all
in the rattling Ramcharger
into town for ice cream cones.
He threw sugar at us
and wondered why
we could not go to bed. Annette
was the worst, her body could not
break it down, the sugar, so she
dissolved. None of us would tell him
this—we loved
Saturday nights too much.

The daughters hunger for the mother,
low in their bellies. When sick,
they call out for her. They hope to swallow
words, the voice in the air, across miles.
They hunger for her in their dreams,
though not for breast or bottle.
For her solid certainty in all things.

But we had to put our clothes away
in the *joor*. We each had one. How
do you spell it? There was no point
in telling me. I couldn't read, but I
knew letters, could recite
the alphabet. I was so angry
when I learned how to spell *drawer*.

Years later, the father took their eyes
with a poker, so that they could not
see him and his new woman.
This from the mother, who

saw all but her own irrelevance.
They did not feel it, cauterization.
Somehow they did not see
the poker on its way.

The rescue party fails
to retrieve her, to pluck
her up and out of her delusions.
In her world, the daughters
have locked her in the tower
high up, windows without glass.
The elements sob their grief,
but she does not try to gain
freedom. She loves the daughters,
three women grown, beyond
measure. Yet she will not call
for them. She will not be a bother.

It was my turn to be the Virgin Mary.
Annette was her sister, Elizabeth. Lisa
had to be John the Baptist. These are
the stories we knew. We never got as far
as Jesus—the women were more interesting.

In those days, everyone smoked—
in restaurants, on airplanes, in elevators.
I learned to breathe it in over the bacon
and eggs at Pappan's after church each Sunday.
Pappy and Grandma and Grandma all
became fire breathers but not Grandma
Josephine, Dad's mom. She never took to it,
and I knew I wouldn't either. We had that
and our chubby faces. And the animals—how
they loved her—the dog, the two cats.
They'd sip air from her fingers—the smoke
filling up their little, little lungs.

At the grocery store, I felt the meat through
plastic. My favorite was the ground beef.
Mommy was so embarrassed—little handprints,
the handled meat, finger holes in the plastic wrap.

She smoked and she smoked
and never grew tired of it.
Ashtrays overflowed and were
emptied, but still she'd shake one
loose from the pack. Always
she bought them by the carton.
They never lasted long.
I didn't know *addiction*, the word
or meaning, but I understood
compulsion. The need to pick
and pick until the nose bled,
all behind the curtain. Hidden
from Mommy but not from the world.

In preschool, I drew myself
as I wanted to be, like Mommy,
with glasses. Also pink eye.
How I loved to peel back
the pus and make piles of it
in the sheets. She never watched.
But the teacher thought
the glasses and the pink circles
were bruises and took me
into the hallway with Mommy.
It smelled like lemon and turpentine
and burned my nose, so clean.
No, Mommy only hits me on the bottom,
when I deserve it. I thought of hangers
but said nothing. I heard my mother's sigh
but could not imagine why.

Color and Sound

When the new job came—
a blessing, Mommy said, who
only worked Saturdays but
stopped—it was the midnight
shift, and everyone needed to be
quiet in the daytime. There were no
more picnics under the table or
over it. We learned to chew without
smacking our lips; though there was
no more pepperoni. Boiled brussels
sprouts that I hid in the stuffing
of the dining room chairs. Sticky
fingers from the slime, but they
were quiet fingers. We did not want
to wake him up.

Lisa began to erase
herself when she was so
small—more hair, dark and curly,
permanently tan skin. Caramel.
It was the wrong color; it was Mommy's
color as a child, she told us.
Lisa began, and then she erased,
redrafting again and again.
She got into the car and told no one.
The dog didn't bark, and we missed her
laughter in the silent summer.
Hot and quiet and no drama, no giggles
and squeaks. She could imitate
any voice—but she could not obey.
She got into the car
without telling Mommy or us.
The police came in the daylight, sirens
announcing danger to the neighborhood.
No one knew what she wore, what she looked
like, where she was playing. I doubled over
with guilt, eating my stomach like a living thing.
My sister. It was my fault
she had gone away.

Do you want a lickin'?
I didn't understand the word.
My tiny self could almost see
the letters before I knew them, before
I could form the cutting words I would
give to my mother in adolescence, broken
bottles of sound. But what was a lickin'?
I imagined it with an o—*lickon*, or something
crabby and scabby—*lichen*? It was not
a soft word, but the smack was always
muted by clothing, the dull thud.
That time, I had crumpled up all her cigarettes.
Oh the money, she screamed. *The waste.*
But I could not tell her I was afraid
when she became the dragon, smoke
blowing through her nostrils.

We did not go camping,
because her idea of roughing
it was the Holiday Inn. So
glib and dry, but she got her way.
Always. We did not go camping,
so we never learned to forage
for nuts and berries. We lie in the forest
at the edge of the desert, choking
on purple stones. She only laughs.

He prepared the pasta each Sunday,
doctored the sauce in the jar into
something passable. Or we went
empty-handed to Pappy and Grandma's
for dinner. Grandma made
the gnocchi herself, simmered
the sauce with sausage and pepperoni for hours.

Ghosts

The dead baby did not haunt us
in the usual ways—there were
no white sheets in the darkness, no
creaky floorboards. She told us at
Christmas one year, showed us, hanging
from the tree: an ornament, round,
an angel inside, wings spread wide.
To commemorate, remember
the small bundle they buried one
day, in someone else's grave. No,
he did not lurk in the shadows
of the too-small house. There was no
room for him. He was still inside
her, and we could not take his place.
He had come first but left—
we had not deserved him. He died
to make room for the unworthy.
God took him from our unkindness.
It was a punishment to know
this, that we were only girls who
didn't deserve the son, the brother.

Is sex so easy now
because it wasn't then?
No one in the house was ever
satisfied. Where did they find
the energy to make us?
It came from a broken place
that cracked open, a baby's
head that could not be put together.

In *Oklahoma*, they lived before Ziploc, before
paper towels. So they wrapped food in cloths
and put the cloths into baskets for picnics.

Mommy washed the lettuce and dried
the leaves with paper towels.
She pressed hamburger patties between
plates with waxed paper. Balls of meat
became flat discs. She knew
how to do everything.
Dad took me to the bakery to get
the buns, and I was so happy—
it was my birthday.

Pappy was allergic
to cucumbers, but
she put them into
salads anyway.
Let him pick them out.
Her father, who allowed
another man to claim
and beat her. He gave her
away to the stepfather first.
Then to my father. Passing her off,
but he liked to brag that he took
her over his knee at twenty-one.
Birthday parties in the spring,
tomato and cucumber salads.
Pappy spitting seeds, turning slowly red.

The slice of light under the bedroom door.
We stood behind it, urging Annette out and
into it. The living room, the muted sounds
of another world: television. We created excuses
for her—she could not sleep, she needed
water, could she go to the bathroom?
We plotted at infuriating him
and wound him up and out, a toy.
The bedroom light would come on, the threat
of lickins. The stern voice.

In one version, the mother
is the soothsayer,
her daughters the harpies.
They could not stop shrieking
their disbelief. Their father
had not met another woman,
not like that. Their father
was the sun in the sky that they
chased on their wings.
And yet, the soothsayer,
without sight, was right.

A mother's love is precious—
not because of its supposed
abundance, but because it can turn
you away from the heart. It can
cast you into the wilderness
for a lifetime without preparation,
supplies, a guide. A mother's love
can dry up like a river in its parched
bed of dirt and dead plants.
We have such rivers in California,
empty things, an occasional trickle.
When you fall into disfavor,
you are nothing.

Our Mother of Sorrows

Because there was no kindergarten in
our suburb, they sent me to Catholic
school, and there I learned we did not go
to church. Sometimes a lady came to Mommy,
who was often resting in a darkened room,
and they spoke about sacraments, Jesus,
and all that. We put the towels on our heads
and took turns pretending to be Mary,
but who knew what *virgin* meant?
Mommy read to us each night about the Holy
Family. She tried to explain:
We are born, and then we grow up and old,
and then we die. And then we do it again?
I asked. No, we go to heaven.
Will you be in heaven, Mommy? Only God knows.
Every time you broke the commandments
was a black mark on your soul. Too many,
and heaven was out of the question.
But will we be in heaven together?
It's how I began to learn
about questions without answers.

Can no one save her,
the mother? Can nothing
be done to bring her back
to earth, to the wet dirt
and flowering impatiens
of the past? The loving mother
is a distant memory, deep.
She must be so cold and lonely,
no glass in the windows. Nothing
sharp to stop the wind and the rain,
gray Pittsburgh, from filling her with air
and lifting her into the clouds. She will float
away believing no one loved her. She disbelieves
the facts, disbelieves in innocence. You have
put her in this prison, too.

Mommy glared at Pappy from her
chair, smoking into our air,
turning the walls yellow as we
watched. There was a program on
the old television about venereal diseases—
living things under the microscope.
I asked: Did you have one of those in the war?
He turned red with shame or anger but answered.
Mommy would not. Her anger was pale.

A mother never gets over
the loss of a child. You know
this so well, without any children—
real or imagined—of your own.
A mother never recovers
her perspective on the world
of pain. All the cuts and scrapes
are the end of all things.
The baby died after a day,
but three little girls, one after
the next, lived. Miracle babies
but not boys. Somehow always
less than, even though we were more.

I was so angry when
they put Daddy's father into
the ground and threw a party:
catered lunch at the church hall,
tables and chairs.
He was gone before my first communion,
which would be celebrated in the same church
hall—white dress and veil and cake. The blessing
on my forehead—was it the one he'd received before
going limp and still?

Dad often brought pizza on Friday
afternoons, before the 3 to 11 shift.
It was a church basement from
their old neighborhood, down
the Rocks. Our Lady of Sorrows,
the pizza, for Our Mother of Sorrows.
She washed the dirt, the sweat
from our little bodies each night.
I helped her bathe my sister
in the sink with the dishes. I kept
the suds from her eyes, pulled
out the forks and knives
before they stabbed her chubby
skin, so fresh and fragile.

The mother never goes away, even when she is silent. Her daughters cannot see, but they know the shape of her, the jagged lines, the breath that fills the room with fire. They feel the heat of her.

The mother languishes in her tower,
a bird and a snake, in the air and of
the earth. She unfolds her love—a flower
that gasps and fades for children. But what does
a mother's love mean for three grown daughters
with feet planted so softly in the dirt
and earth? They live in the world and have fought
for their cemetery plots, breath of hurt
in dirt. The mother is the snake again
and will slither and haunt even those plots.
A mother's love has no peace. It began
so long ago, with the father. Those thoughts
swelled and grew and rounded. Then the mess came.
The surgeon's knife, then the squeals, without shame.

Oh, my mother of sorrows.
The pizza's here, from the church
in the old neighborhood where Italians
have slowly been replaced
by the Blacks, Grandma said.
Exodus as trickle, thinning blood.
But old women still go
to the church basement each Friday
to bake the pizza that opens the doors
and keeps them opened. Red sauce,
only a sprinkle of cheese.

It's quiet, because Mommy is in bed,
resting. There will be no more babies.
Cancer, they said—the word spread
through the family. And so she rested
in darkened daylight, and we ate
pizza alone. The sacrifices
you make for blood.

Cracked Chair

You break the chair
over my back each time
we speak. I hear you pause,
smoking, even though you quit.
I hear the words whistle
when you pick up the chair
before the snap, the crack
of your tongue as you destroy me.
I grew up thinking Italians
all broke chairs,
but it was always only you.

Once Dad won the lottery
and built the house a deck—
fresh wood with roof and skylight,
furniture for watching the rain.
It was her favorite place. She
smoked and smoked in the rain,
one breath after the other.
We played cards in summertime.
We made Pappy his coffee in the
nice, new mug. Lisa always won,
rummy. The baby of the family.
Spoiled, like Pappy—the youngest
and youngest son.
I could almost forget how much
I hated home. Mommy could too.

We drove at midnight to the ocean,
an impossible journey from Pittsburgh,
but Dad drove through mountains
in the dark while we slept. Mommy held
the map with a flashlight. And so we went
and misbehaved together.
We packed the cooler and filled it
with sandwiches. Fruit. A carton of hardboiled
eggs with rings around the yolks.
Juice drinks for us should we wake.
She shook us every time we stopped
for gas: bathroom time. We only stopped
to fill the tank, not to empty ours.

The store was in the town, not in our suburb.
Dad told us that some of the old people buying cat
food ate it themselves. We were lucky girls
who ate meat cooked on the grill. Those
old people probably lived all alone, he said.
That's a hard thing.

Did Dad ever live alone, I wondered? There was his time
in the service, but that could not have been very
solitary. And he would never live alone—
when Mom finally left after thirty-four years, he found another
lady.

She's not as pretty as Mommy, or so Pappy said.
I didn't meet her for years and years. She was
a friend, first. How replaceable women are—
if only he had upgraded sooner. Like when Mommy
let the laundry climb to the ceiling and through the roof.
She was always so very tired—too tired to haul all
the dirty clothes to the basement. This was
after she came back from the hospital; she was

gone for so long. Dad and Pappy brought us to the bus
stop an hour early, and we had to stand there, pretending
it was fine, it was normal. Our hair grew tangled
into knots, and it hurt when Dad tried to brush them out.
She was gone, and they wouldn't say when
she was coming home. They didn't know,
I understood later. It took me so long to piece it all
together, to understand that Mommy and Daddy
were not to be repeated in my own life.

The father has plucked out
their eyes, or else her daughters would
see her, save her. She is in the dungeon
of her own making,
the finished basement of the old house,
the brick albatross around her neck,
a collar. She will leave and take
the furniture while he is at work—
or so he says. While he's somewhere else,
not with her in the shadows
of the laundry room,
standing on concrete.

All the fevers I gave myself at school
because Mommy was so sick. All the stomachaches
that never tired. She was gone and we ate
burned chicken for dinner. I hated the way
everything Daddy made was black with char.
Well done, he said.

She's there in the valley of the shadow,
hiding from us, though we are blind and can't
see her footsteps in the desert that binds
us together. She is the shadow. No.
She is the desert, and we are thirsty.

There is the truth now, in the spines
of the cactus that towers above us all,
the cactus that creates our shared shadow.
We push her hand through its spines:
she is a weapon of torture, a device, so like

her advice to us as children, not to lie
with boys before our time. Make them wait,
and then make them wait more. Men will have
their whores, she says from the shadow.
Look at you.

On the beach,
the sand was
her ashtray. She
lay beneath the umbrella,
smoking. It was so much
like home, except the sun.
The sound of the ocean,
the smell of it. No blinds.
There were sunglasses and
umbrellas and interminable
cigarettes, but it was not home.
I took long walks and rejoiced.

You should be grateful
no one ever cracked
a chair over your back.
Your father never punched
through your face like the plaster
of a wall, holes everywhere.
He did the one time.
Because I wrote that I hated you.
The word has ever been a scourge.
Black and blue for a week—no one
said anything. Did anything.
He ripped the pages.
You're not a writer.
Yes, I am.

The mother handed her a stack of gauze
and told her to clean herself between her legs.
The daughter was bleeding, but no baby came.
The endless stream and leak of blood.
The mother put her into the bathroom stall
and warned her not to sit on the seat.
The bathroom was the private place,
the space of stories and silence.

Lisa

My father predicted the toe tag
for Lisa—the permanence of ending.
He had a way with his words
that made you look away. He would
say the unsayable, and no one could
stuff it back down his narrow throat.
And he was usually wrong.
She had only gotten into the car
with Pappy—gone for ice cream. Each
the baby of the family.
She had only swallowed the pills—
she did it just for show, so we'd know
she was serious. It was inconvenient
to visit her in the psychiatric hospital
after work. The gaping maw of her need
struck me in the face, silent.
There was no way to feed her.
But her toenails were painted pretty pink.

Into this hospital, into that hospital,
Lisa disappeared. An arm there, a leg
in State College. Indiana took the rest
of her. The ring of bruises at her throat,
the bad man. Dad again
predicted the toe tag, but there was nowhere
to hang it. Everything had been erased. Smudged.

Mommy went to visit the first time,
but no more. She did what she had done before:
took to her bed while I washed all the dishes
we owned and stacked them to the kitchen ceiling,
wet and dripping. Rinsed clean of her sin.

At some unknowable point,
Mommy became Mom. Or Mother,
to scold. Daddy became Dad, never
Father. She is Mother now,
a title, a descriptor.
Nothing more.

Lisa erased her limbs,
and I drew them in.
Charcoal. Messy. Smudged
like the bruises from the bad man
she could not do
without. I drew her legs
crooked so she couldn't stand,
couldn't walk back to him.
But it did no good. She took
her eraser and stole
my charcoal. She drew
the lines faint, to match
her new personality.

Pull the pasta up and out
of your throat, make it whistle
between your teeth as it whips
through the gap. Un-eat your
dinner and be good. In my dreams,
we are in the old house on Oakbine
Avenue, and you are still married.
I'd yank up my dinner every
night to make it true.

The mother goes to church and makes spaghetti,
leaving the hermitage for the outer world.
She is the old lady who keeps her church
open—no one wants to pray when they
can meditate nondenominationally. But people
from the neighborhood come for pasta.
They scrape paper plates clean with fork and knife,
the crusts of bread if they're Italian. The father does not
come, no longer frequents church basements.
But the mother has provided, has nourished.
In this, she is happy.

He says he was afraid—
the father afraid of the mother.
How she'd shriek above him,
wake him into the depths
of her dark eyes. The harpy
without her wings. Hovering
hands above his neck, she fluttered
with rage. He used to beat her, she says.
A collar of bruises round her neck,
a cage, she says. Oh the fear
and dread of them both.

Mommy as Snake

You humble yourself.
You apologize.
I'm sorry I thought you were crazy,
it's just that I've always
loved Dad more.
You are the snake in the grass,
overgrown worm from the desert.
I should have believed your truth,
believed in the Other Woman,
but I could not. Blinded
by faith, I would not eat
the apple. It is the mother's foot
on my back, crushing me.

The snake's trick, in this small garden,
is silence. *Leave the snake alone*, the father
warns, but you are tempted. The pink impatiens
border the ugly beige brick of the house, the
slag driveway where the cars are parked. The silent
snake sees it all and calls out to no one. The new
family paces the walk and climbs the stoop, a block
of concrete before the door. The snake sits
in the flowers, cool and patient.

My mother keeps a list
of my sins against her,
the ways in which I've wronged her,
tucked beneath her bra strap,
with the money. She pays in cash
while I sip bourbon from a juice glass
with Christ emblazoned across it
three thousand miles away. Not
from *home*, because home is where
the heart is. Mine is with the bourbon
and the ocean. California. My mother
takes the list out to recite through
the long distance, but sand comes out
of her mouth. There's no blood
left inside her. She is a worm
in the sand, a destroyer.

The father hates the mother
but loves you. Hates
the shrillness of women politicians
but loves you, because you are
quiet. But the mother was quiet,
for a long time, smoking in the dark
room, blinds drawn. The father
warns you against snakes and apples.
But you want the tart taste,
the snake a sage. You want advice.
A broken rib from each parent made you,
and you've never let them alone since.
You must have them both: the father
who hates the mother, and the mother
who hates you.

The bourbon with the hand-
written label, very small batch,
is the only way to stop her voice
inside me. I can't pour perfectly
and some slips down the side
of the glass. Water back. Like
the movies. A perfect complement
to the mashed potatoes, fried eggs.
Cook what you can.
Mother yourself.

Unbearable, and yet. Here it is.

Hide the poems
and bury them in the ground—
put dirt in the envelope
and crush them together.

Put them in the grave
with Mommy, so she can read
through the dirt. Oh, the mother.

She gave it all, so she can take it all.

We will return to dust,
to dusk, to the liminal
and in-between. But
the mother has cursed
the daughters to hear
her voice, even in the dirt.
There is no escape.

We put people into boxes
called coffins, where they lie
lifeless and still. I practiced
after Dad's father died. This
is the last breath. No. This
is it. Hands still and at
the sides, but my chest
kept moving, lungs demanding
air, and my lips would part
against my will. I was seven.
Just practicing for the main event.

My greatest love,
my greatest enemy.
That is what it means
to be a mother. No one
else can cut straight
to bone, through skin
and fat and muscle
and veins. No one can
slice so cleanly to what
holds you up. Oh,
the Mother. Our Lady
of Anatomy. Where
is her heart?

Oh, Mommy is a snake, but I want her.
She planted impatiens in her garden
crouching low, hands deep in dirt, she planted
what would grow. A border to our sad home.

She planted impatiens in her garden
each year. It was an anniversary
that would grow. A border to our sad home.
She hung the laundry to dry on the deck.

Each year, it was an anniversary;
she refused what others would celebrate.
She hung the laundry to dry on the deck
and hid in bed, curtains drawn against us.

She refused what others would celebrate,
crouching low, hands deep in dirt. She planted.
She hid in bed, curtains drawn against us.
Oh, Mommy is a snake, but I want her.

Will they lower her into the earth,
her face round and embalmed? Puffy,
with a resolute, "she looked good"?
Or will the burned bits of her scatter,
ash to choke on? The body is so much
to throw away. One cigarette after the next,
stained her fingers, stained our walls.
Soon, she will be the stain, the rot in soft earth—
the ash that sticks in your throat.

When you make a mess,
sometimes the only thing
is to wipe the table clean.
Lean into it as you push
the plates to the floor,
the butter dish. Let
the dishes break. Let
the dog come for the scraps
before you take the broom
and push everything out the door.

Acknowledgments

The following poems (listed by first line) appeared in *Prairie Schooner*:

It was her knees I loved
There was always some man lying
She smoked and she smoked
Lisa began to erase
Do you want a lickin'?
The dead baby did not haunt us
Dad often brought pizza on Friday

I'd also like to thank Jason Irwin, Madelynn Dickerson, and Tarrah Krajnak for their help with this manuscript. Special thanks to Tarrah for the hours we spent laying the poems down on her sunlit table, culling, and trying to get the order just right.

Thanks also to the following people (in no particular order) for believing in this project: Phil Taggart, Marsha de la O, David Starkey, Sharon Venezio, Kim Dower, Gabrielle LeMay, Mary Kay Rummel, Friday Gretchen, Stacy Russo, Jeff Phillips.

About the Author

Nina Clements earned an MFA in creative writing from Sarah Lawrence College. Her poems have appeared in *The Santa Barbara Literary Journal*, *The Penn Review*, and *Prairie Schooner*. She works as a librarian in Madison, Wisconsin.